Animals Live Everywhere

Joan Thompson
Illustrations by Wendy Edelson

HAMPTON-BROWN

Animals live everywhere. Some
live in snug, hidden places. Some
live in high-up places. Some live
where people live. Some roam free
in places where there aren't a lot
of people.

2

Look for animals everywhere you
go. You may see some that you
didn't know were there.

Animals live in houses. Some are
in plain sight. Some are in cracks
and small holes.

Look, and you may see them.

4

A goldfish swims round in a small bowl.

A cat snuggles by the fire.

A spider spins a web by the window.

And somewhere a mouse is hiding.

Animals live in backyards. Some are in the grass. Some are on a pretty plant. One lives in his own little house.

Look, and you may see them.

A dog smacks
a ball.

A rabbit nibbles
sweet peas.

A butterfly sits on a
snapdragon.

And somewhere a snail is hiding.

Animals live in the park. Some
are on the small lake. Some are on
the swings. Some are in deep holes.
Look, and you may see them.

A swan swims across the lake.

A pigeon snacks on bread and seeds.

A squirrel sits on a swing and begs for a peanut.

And somewhere a snake is hiding.

Animals live at the beach.
Some are in the sand. Some are
in the waves. Some are in snug,
rocky places.

Look, and you may see them.

A gull sweeps
down to grab
a fish.

A dog sniffs at a
crab in the sand.

A seal bobs on the
swelling waves.

And somewhere clams are hiding.

Animals live in the forest. Some
are in rotted logs. Some are in
creeks. Some are in small places
tucked out of sight.

Look, and you may see them.

A blue jay looks
for a bite to eat.

A raccoon fishes
in the creek.

An owl sleeps in
a tree.

And somewhere a deer is hiding.

Animals live on farms. Some are in the barn. Some are in the grassy fields. Some are even under the farmer's house!

Look, and you may see them.

A cow grazes on sweet grass.

A pig wallows in the smelly mud.

A lamb drinks from a milk pail.

And somewhere a kitten is hiding.

Animals really do live everywhere: in houses and backyards, in parks and beaches, in forests and on farms. They live in many different places.

Look, and you may see them, but then . . . maybe you won't!